X-Ray and the Pull of Poetry

Selected Poems by Joan Sibley

Edited by Martha Herbert Izzi
and Penelope Weiss

ONION RIVER PRESS

Burlington, Vermont

Text © 2021 by Joan Sibley

All rights reserved. No part of this publication may be reproduced, distributed, or transmitted in any form or by any means, including photocopying, recording, or other electronic or mechanical methods, without the prior written permission of the publisher, except in the case of brief quotations embodied in critical reviews and certain other noncommercial uses permitted by copyright law.

Onion River Press
191 Bank Street
Burlington, VT 05401

ISBN: 978-1-949066-70-8

Introduction

> "I named him X-Ray:
> unerring imager
> of my inner being,
> exact examiner
> of my private wars."
> —Joan Sibley

Joan Sibley was born on February 17, 1939, in Worcester, Massachusetts, a daughter of privilege and Victorian manners. In her youth she was a student at Boston University. Robert Lowell was one of her teachers. She once casually admitted that Sylvia Plath and Ann Sexton were in her class.

Joan lived reclusively in her cabin deep in the woods on a dirt road in Shrewsbury, Vermont, a small rural town in the Green Mountains, where she had lived for most of her adult years. All manner of wildlife were her friends and closest companions. These creatures appear in many of her poems, often fused with the deepest part of her consciousness and the truths she could never express in any other way.

Joan died in her cabin on December 16, 2013, on a winter night two months short of her 75th birthday. It came as a surprise to the people who knew her, but in recent conversations, and in her writing, it seems she anticipated her own death.

Only a few days before that night, she had come, as she usually did, to our small poetry writing group at the local library in Shrewsbury. That she had joined the writing group was a surprise, probably even to herself.

At that last meeting, she was uncharacteristically at ease after a year of meetings. She had read with a new confidence a wonderful poem that left us all feeling as though she would remain in the group and, perhaps, had reached a new level of inner peace.

We found many of her early poems when we went with her executor into the cabin months after her death. There we found a trove of books and her extensive writings, dating back to when she was 18. There was an old manual typewriter, no television, no computer. There was a radio, a desk and shelves of books of poetry and literature, wildlife and nature writing, classics. There was an on-going Scrabble game, a score card showing "thee and me."

As we began to read her work, we were again astonished at her range and imagery. Her poetry is sometimes raw, sometimes funny, often heart-breaking. Her reticent demeanor bore little resemblance to the strong, poignant, mischievous, often brilliant poet that she was. She had a camera into her soul.

To our knowledge, except for four early poems ("Fireplay," "Lost," "Sandfall," and "Shadow,") published in the literary magazine of Stephens College, Columbia, Missouri in 1957, Joan never sent poems to any publishers, friends or other poets. This collection is a selection of 66 poems spanning Joan's life from 18 to 74. We hope you enjoy it.

Martha Herbert Izzi & Penelope Weiss

Contents

Fireplay	1
Lost	3
Sandfall	5
Shadow	7
The Doll's Speech	9
At the Wind's End	12
Slow But Sure	16
School of the Deer Ride	17
The White Giant Moth of Winter	20
Leaf Birds	22
X-Ray and the Pull of Poetry	24
Starting Over	26
An Inhuman Life	28
From Lines That Came to Me in Sleep	30
Indian Doll	32
July	35
On Otter Creek August 17, 2002	37
Hideout	41
Confessions of Jonah's Wife	43
The Sheep	47
Going from Door to Door	50
Real Estate Needs	53
The Hermit Said	57
Immaculate Glide of Summer	58
Meadow's Child	60
Said Pond	62

The Blackstone: A Diary	65
Unicorn Field	71
When the Forest Walks	72
Wish List	74
Also Ran: The Truth	77
Half a Prayer, Version 2	78
Antithesis	80
Beside the Millhouse	82
Hope	85
Road Walk	86
The Old Woman Cries	90
Who Am I?	91
A Dream in December	93
A Lasting Image of Ears, Version 2	95
August Again	96
Round in Summer's Eye	98
In the Gratzel Store	100
Sighting: After an Old Friend's Death	102
The Road Back	104
Visiting	106
A Swimming Hole Would Be Nice	108
As Birds are Words for Water	109
The Blue Ribbon	111
Fern	113
Flower Lesson	115
For Now	116
Forecast	118
Heddi	119

Hunting Season and a Meeting Remembered	121
Identical Coiffures	124
Little Grass Ghost	126
"Montana"	127
Nice Cane	131
Reunion Near the Sea	135
Someone's Gram	137
Walking the Lake	141
Who Is the Child	144
X-Ray Revisited or, One Hen's Dilemma	146
Sing to Me: A Poem of Regret	148
Destination: Birds	149

FIREPLAY

After a sun and work day
The child in her went walking.
Anywhere appeared
Where a man of the railroad put a match
To the smoked cigars and candy wraps
Of people catching trains.
He treks daily from the depot,
Sets barrel rust a-reddening,
Returns.
Inside, he rocks his unknown sadness to sleep.

She added sticks
And watched for long and warmed her hands—
The bittersweet sticks became as bloodworms
Living in a painted season.
By inner swells of breathing red and softing,
A colony of heartflares
Beat out the life of their township.
An altar town.
The flame of its living, the smoke of its dying
Burn the stranger, and linger on her clothes.
The bloodworm villagers light their mission town,
And spark the young eye with empathy.
Through eyes of child and not of child she sees them.

Smile of eighteen
May end her sun and cloud day
In a smokerest dream.
Berries of the bittersweet
Are tastes forgotten,

Burned away.
The bloodworms know.
Through sooted pane she sees
His ever-nod; and her fingers curve warm
In the crispness.
Experience is the beholden.
Soon she will see them smoldering sorrowless.
The bloodworms live and die
In their own painted seasons.
After a sun and work day
She had a little fireplay
And the woman in her went home.

Autumn 1957

LOST

She walks in the night.
Comes the chill, melting lime air
Reminding umber walls
Of moss and dust.
Darkened freeze of green,
Remain, and as a breath of Satan falls,
Remain, remain
While the alley gasps; then stills
In swoon of September.

She halts in the night.
"Crush, crush my sun-touched pearls
Shadowed in a tree-dark sky.
Soon shall I ascend
The earthbound glory mound!"
Cry of a heroine, lost cry.

Comes a leaf
And a scratch-path stops in yellow dust
On the paving.
Summer's verdant, young dependence past;
Then, one creation, printed miniature
In an autumn alley.

"Swing, swing off your hinges
And crumble starry in my arms!
Forever must I call?
I am not invisible in ironed night!
Or could I be?"
Child heroine,

Try trampling, trampling
Your enemy soldiers' grass blades.
Walk the earth a little,
Heroine.

1957

SANDFALL

Where can I run?
In peasant blouse loose, open, so thin—
In Grecian skirt, lovely in light,
comforting folds …
I am waiting,
Pouring from a shell scoop eager sand.
But in my shell scoop, there is Tom.

Pale sky fish silvers the sea,
Wind, wind blows it inland to me
Sitting on the sea wall,
Loving you,
Night of southern spring.

Let me walk across the ocean,
Beyond the pyramid of rolling, rolling light
Into that dark and cloudy moon's escape,
Over unseen line of sea and sky,
To my soft, soft isle of infancy
Where I, young woman now,
May stand in soundless, silver past blue.

Night, you have put my folks to sleep
Under mossy trees and flower smells;
Another breath, my home earth, faraway
Will soon hush you.
But I shall stay awake tonight,
And set my fear upon the sand.
What is in the sky?
An arrow drawn back, back

By his night hand, a half-myth left alone,
Into the forward flowing sap
Of many midnight clouds.
Something in the sea wind calls,
And I'm running!

A cloud chaser I, a piece of the sky.
I run,
But in my shell scoop, there is Tom.

1957

SHADOW

You were gone.
While a sun-soft thing
In the dusk-flaked elms
Of the settling realms
Hummed feather tunes for me,
An older shadow came and whispered in my ear,
"Anytime."
Night discovered me.

You were gone.
Still elms
There was peace in your brown bodies,
And arms hung out their mourning
Blue in blue.

Moon-polished pines on the hill,
You seemed a womanly row,
All glowing,
As my dreamself, in its aching and reaching,
Saw you,
And struggled not to fall.
"Anytime."

Now in a soft, free hush of dawn
The elms in faint green hope
Awake me.
This early mellowland, serenely kind.

But oh, you were gone,
And I need your human strength!

"Anytime."
Bitter breakfast nut
Swallow me,
For I see starched leaves
And a dirty glass sky.

1957

THE DOLL'S SPEECH

I
In the twentieth year she came,
A visitor to life on her own doorstep.
A wicker chair in lantern rhythm spell
Rocked upon the porch as if in pain.
Long she'd rested in its arms
In the sudden angularity of children;
Many times its grudging grumble heard
Like a comfort, or a distant train.
But as a trellis checkered black
The splintered boards of August eve,
At last she only saw it there—
Sunken cushion, button gone.
Old seasons whispered under the light;
More of them than she ever knew.

As she went country hillward home,
Sun sleeping on her back like an orange cat,
She left no trace along the trail
Of cartwheels she'd been turning
Out of childhood,
One between each half-grown shoe,
Anymore than the rains and green wagons
Draw long reminders of themselves
When it is summer.

Oh drifting lily snows
Along the road
Once more

Under her feet it moves with her,
Hushed white tape,
While from an unsaid blade of grass
A cricket daughter murmurs once,
Innocent and distant as a doll deceased.
It is here she stops to listen for her past,
And it ravels round,
Holds her the doll,
And makes her wise.

II
"Good night" of the mending-mouth women,
Patchers of quilt and coiffure,
Their harp string voices lingering
In the tapestried dusk of a parlor.
She hears, on the porch,
In washday window curtains,
And bathes, and waits.
As when the merry clothesline swung in spring,
And she hid until the allee-allee-in-free
Or the bell for lunch; as when
The day was one burst apple
And she saw in the streets
The browse of old men; as when
She slippered on a sifting sea of spruces,
Away from the stolen candy scene;
Under her feet it moves with her…

At nobody noon she is small,
Poised on the promise of the day;
Fields are far away as a different time.
But then she stepped upon the shell

Of a robin's egg. At home they said "Oh,"
And "Good night" to each other,
Much, to her, as when she'd made
Courteous inquiry of a full-blown rose,
That only nodded,
As one went out into the afternoon.

1959

AT THE WIND'S END

Still astride the wheels of the season,
I callous into sampler fitness,
A broadcloth image my mother will sew
Of Berthold's good and country daughter,
Anonymous as any soil-scented sloven.
But while the earth deepens,
And boulder clouds shut down the mill of day,
I scrape no word for bumpkin boys.
All else now in the sky is dim;
And I remember him.
My eyes travel with his rippling brown smiles—
Two pebbles wink, referents to and reverence
Of another day in this gentle, voicing field,
Where now the red McCormick rolls
His backward glances toward me,
And I am wind in the furrows,
In the long summer valleys of our love.

It was August, and in pinafore dusts
I ran scattering laughs and limbs all
For the world of a sun-turvy grin.
Oh the refluent earth is smiling
Where I grind gears at the row's end;
I feel a drop of rain.
It was here, that day,
On the tippling minnow waters of the land,
That he smiled at the wind's end and dipping turn,
His need and his surprise.
Too soon it was like sleep I gave him.
And he, he gave me sleep—

But never more open epitaph
Than this always August field.

The corn and he had grown tall last summer,
Had ripened in my sight,
While all the long days long
Men toiled, and his shoulders broadened, like theirs.
While I lingered in the skirts of spring
Unopened, I saw him in the early summer,
Saw him with the men on raw plantations,
Saw him stamp the earth.

Surely this lonely day
Speaks to me,
As when I could not listen,
When the muscled hills and sinewed woods
Held me in a simple vision of his being.
I remember stone walls roamed far
Beneath his hand.

When we burst into first gold,
The young haycocks,
Rural pyramids of the farm's estate,
Filtered their spiced haloes
Into the kingdom of our love.

My many-forked and fighting days
Were wheeling suns and reaches
For apple gold in his neighbor earth,
On the other side of his walls.
I had not thought what his words to me
Could be, but only knew they could not be

Surprising, nor less easy than the streams
Through which he moved in toil.
I feared my own ungracious wood,
Some foreign oak, if we should speak;
A better fence, I pulled the wind around me.
And he built his walls—away from me?
In truth we were in no way
Each to the other, strange;
Except in the common one that passes.
I think how even in his struggle
He traced the forest fields,
Brown and shirtless over greenafar,
Where sun shining air sung into him
The music of the long deer's run.

My days of veiled and silent angels
Were his days, too. This was all to be
Transformation into gold: Caught
In a smile like leaves, the falling light,
Eyes that did not see their searching,
And could not turn to me for long.
We in lonely orchards
Cried through branching prison bars.

He might have made me daisy chains
From bright and white-starred clusters,
And in clover-ridden cradles
I would have whispered thanks.
But that fawn escaping fawnhood
Could lay no milky necklace on my throat.
And I forgave my dread.
I forgave,

At once the spring was faint,
Almost fainted away,
Until one day I ventured further out,
He saw me, wind's end,
And the earth and I were one,
And it was my summer.

Gone were spring and the days
When black over the sun came
The jeering of the crows,
My mother cawing mealtime from the house,
The limping wings that turned my days to rain,
When I was a lamb in the sheeping folds.

Today I ride the rake
Across an hour.
Tall grew the corn,
Green was the hour.
A week went by, and then
His lungs collapsed forever.

It is darkening now. Across the hills
Torn flights of blackbirds weave
Dreamless through the ochre skies.
He has sunk in a withering dusk,
And I ride the rake across an hour.
A splinter in my hand reminds me
Of today and of tomorrow.

1960

SLOW BUT SURE

Slow but sure
The birds ate up spring
Last year,
And now they toss
Melodious mementoes,
Like fruits,
Mellow and hurting
From the long elapse
Into great baskets
Of unruly April wind.

In the wind streams
They've a challenge
And the condescension.
I see hummingbirds
And sparrow-necks
Fruit-flinging,
Defiant,
Impossible,
Like the contradictions
Of planned pleasure
And genuine joy!

Summer, 1960

SCHOOL OF THE DEER RIDE

Children astride a statue wild and leaden,
We pulled at antlers
As late sun saddened the lawn into a vast expanse,
And willow twigs glided in their sheaths of gold.
Hot and damp,
We beat the cold flanks
Until the far brick house was great with darkness.
We dismounted. Yesterday hung in the willow.
Its light released the deer. He moved.
Too suddenly we laughed and ran, ran away!

But we had trespassed there,
Upon the unknown old man's estate,
And knew we would return.
We knew it,
As with the swift oars of our arms
We feathered in the hill's tide
Its milkweed crests too gently topping
As it rolled us in the ships of ourselves
Down to the dark harbor,
Where the builders waited with nails.

In the village that night our mothers
Clamped us into bed
And told us
To sleep between their laundered sails,
And laid them softly over us,
Told us
To drift in these boats they'd made
And their long blue love would rock us

Until a far, far raising of sails.
They sealed us with a last hammered kiss.
So pinning us like baggage to their dreams
That then and there we were forsaken;
So dropping the sails of our riding
That, lost, we dared.

Again we dared the deer,
Although he stood in beauty
Almost suspended from our reach,
As we grasped the mound of his withers.
He held, a color of gloom
Gathered into sculpture, proud
In the sinking grass
And the close, shivered echoes of the leaves
In the nearing woods and ever nearer willow.
                He stood in beauty;
His antlers struck the air
In an absolute but delicate resistance
Against our leaning;
We teased him with a strength of wonder.

Our bodies swung from him
And our laughter ran through us
Directly as the actual sun,
As the quick sighs of the leaves,
So rushing to their utter ends
That we never knew we heard,
Repeated silence with a sound.
                He stood in beauty; it was then
Our legs against his glimmered sides
Sent shining into motion. And we rode

Until yesterday hung in the willow.

But did not know that yesterday,
That trespass to the deer,
Would always hold in half-light
Behind the harbors of our concern;
That near our cautious acts and careful loves
A holiday of light relents
Forever upon the cold dark deer;
That of the lawn around that iron stance
Against our joy and fear,
Deep green abides, moves the cloven feet.
While the lawnlight in inches
Sank holy and sliding,
We knew it as ours.

1969, begun much earlier

THE WHITE GIANT MOTH OF WINTER

The white giant moth of winter
Has settled down to rest.
Down under him
The heart of Christmas lies,
In deeper stillness, cold.
Deep in many Christmases
The old undecorated pine
Sings slowly in his bark
Of the touch of snow.

The white rabbit waits,
Softly, to be lost.
It is his camouflage against the fox.
For it is an ever-present wound he seeks;
It is, in the womb of Christmas,
His wedding that he desires.
Slowly, as he crouches closer, closer
To himself, distances expand.
As the snowlight gathers him into its beyond,
Eyes from all around
Hide the groping of the bodies
With the dim green of their penetration.
Shelter! the animals cry.
They eyes burn colder.
But all the winter night
Gapes at last through the rabbit's eyes.
The whole countryside is relieved
Of the vicious emerald stare, for his
Is a true marriage to his woundedness.
No eyes can see him now,

For all eyes are his.
The fox's mouth dries in envy,
As he circles in the moon-sliver dark,
Snow-blind. His motions crack like death,
His fur stiffens in the wind;
A red rigor mortis, it flies up and stays.
His eyelids shut, he is mange on sticks
The rabbit whimpers.
The night in its roundest hour
Encloses the earth into being with its listening.
The rabbit whines.
At last the earth dark shining
Opens, and is afraid.

Only the great pine, like a god,
Tremendous in his bark's decrepitude, sings.

1970

LEAF BIRDS

Up there on the high pasture,
peninsula in the sky,
the winter tree's bird flock perched
integral as its roots, as still,
on limbs all bent east by the westwind;
branch-black birds at twig ends,
statues on a straining ship's prow.

But when I came too close
they all burst out,
driven by the wind of their wills,
leaving the tree once again leafless.

I think how the gods I always need
are only crippled folk like me,
and yet how a word of praise or recognition
from one of them
can seem to create me, the way the birds
give the winter tree a dark version of spring.
When such a word stands poised on my brain's
   curve,
how loving and how trusting I become!
Like a child inside my aging bones
I long to pull the word down off its perch,
a fragile bit of baby fluff, my first bird,
and cradle it a long time in my hand;
even as I watch the snow-laden sky
that took the vulnerable flock away

from its compliment to the tree,
hide every bird entirely from my sight,
quicker than a drowning.

January 11, 1988

X-RAY AND THE PULL OF POETRY

Each morning my rooster
crowed my rest away at dawn.
Only half awake,
I'd still be in whatever dream
I'd just been having.
When we lose a dream,
too deep-sandwiched
between the fat slices
of sleep and sleep,
sometimes, hours later,
an echo of its voice.
But this was here and now.
I'd be aware! and
long afterwards, remember.

I came to blame the rooster
for my nightmares.
I came to thank him
for the yellow wheel
of the sunflower face
that grew before my eyes
until it burst my dream
in a jaunty blast
of cocka-doodle-doo.

I named him X-Ray:
unerring imager
of my inner being,
exact examiner
of my private wars.

This bird in multi-hues
of reddish tan was quite
a little more to me
than mere alarm clock.
He stood more like a god.

"There are no gods on earth," you say.
"But there are Members of the Board
who gather everyone they can
into the company's great enterprise;
assign each soul a public face."

I was seldom in the office, though.
Often I was miles away from home,
as when I drove my car cross-slope
on a highway 4,000 feet up,
somewhere in the land of Douglas firs.
To my immediate left, about thirty
housecats were coming out of culverts
beneath a stone retaining wall.
Their homes had been in the valley
far, far below.

They'd decided to go wild
and X-Ray, at work
precisely on time,
had awakened me
to this same possibility.

June 3-8, 2013

STARTING OVER

As I drove east on Kelly Stand Road
an owl drew a tipped bowl's curve
from forest roof to windshield view;
grazed glass with wing. A swerve
onto my route made it his province,
and I was second to this joking fellow.
He led me, sailing his long channel
seemed made for him; climbed at last
out over the canopy, his high meadow,
and was lost to me in an instant,
in a green cumulus I couldn't follow!

But what if that vanishing act were mine?
And all inflexible traffic of my kind?
Then, pale young shoots pushing gravel
into loosely-breaking mounds,
huge force in tiny form
transforming to grease-dark shadow
the hulks of our old wheeled animals,
and to uncertain memory their too-certain roads
(they'll growl no more in their steel hides,
as buckshot webs their glass eyes);
thrusting us to the air aisles above,
fun-ride avenues for raptors off-duty
flyways!

For perhaps a motherhood of seasons
we might sleep,
and dream this glad nonsense of owls
making heyday of our reasons;

until the new trees rising
meet the woodland's crown,
and the human child of our yearning wakes
in a pathless haunt of birdfoolery and song
and calls it, fearless, home.

1990

AN INHUMAN LIFE

"How old is she?" I ask,
as I lean to caress
a baby in her bassinette.
She is so tiny, she could be
a blonde cocker spaniel puppy,
a little muffin like Mom's was,
when I was just a child myself,
wanting all the hugs and pats
lavished on him. I could hold
this five-inch human life
in the palm of one hand.

"Six months," her mother surrogate,
a long ago friend of mine whose mind
is half-deranged, although she had
five fine children of her own,
responds. "But she was unable
to grow." My mind gropes
for possible diseases, injury,
for the corn borer who made
a wrong turn into her brain;
but my hand keeps petting her
in a timeless repetition, like waves,
until, lying on my back now,
I see, crawling along my chest
toward my face, a bug as big
as a chipmunk, but richly furred
in black and orange stripes of tiger,
colors that glow as if a sunset
had found them out. The creature

is eyeless, scoop sockets bone white.
Now the thin, black antennae;
now the long, black legsticks,
right-angled at the midpoints,
with felted pinhead tips reaching,
touch my cheeks, my mouth.

I keep stroking, stroking, stroking
the bright, soft fur of tiger,
never having noticed at all
when the human baby turned
into this monster; not feeling
the horror of this transformation.
So tenderly I go on nurturing
this creeping beast of unrelatedness,
this wayward blindness whose intent
is to devour my only, sunrisen life.

October 28, 2004

FROM LINES THAT CAME TO ME IN SLEEP

Although I am engaged in chasms
with this bent work, I may go on
planting a garden for butterflies
that they and I alone will know.
No other humans near. Sunlight
that warms their wings for flight
cannot penetrate a heart so darkened
to the common city struggles of my kind,
and I will suffer the desert
of these flower and mimic insect petals,
of nectared velvet cup and marksman proboscis
that mean life itself to each other.

And yet, so often before now, I've known
a term of beauty unopposed, in which
these flown petals, these fastened wings
make magic of uncertainty, and
tortoiseshell, marigold, sulphur, hibiscus
so take me into their vermilion realms,
my soul at last assumes their very shapes;
and then I am, for all my wrongs, such light,
the garden is my only stay against the grave.

>   Will I fly, too fragile to remain,
>   to lichen-covered hills of Labrador?
>   Will Conscience, heaviest of ladies,
>   sitting cross-footed on an arbor bench—
>   She, witness to her poet
>   thrown out of doors
>   to its proportionate stare,

its merciless, unpeopled shrine,
clap her fat hands to see me go?

Fixed at the crux
of mid-grown and weightless,
of childish and no more,
the hatchy horses race
round the Labrador track.
While Conscience relaxes
back home in the garden,
a fritillary on her nose,
no longer nursing
her feeling of being usurped—
She, with her superior mind!—
to justify my injured psyche's ends,
I, crippled, ride bareback
my wilderness dreams
forever hatching
around and around and around
the oval confines of my hell,
while someone, somewhere
guards me still, lest I
and all the bright chestnut horses
drop off the edge of the world.

February 29, 2004 (revised March 4 and March 6, 2004)

INDIAN DOLL

No young child could love a doll
any more than I loved Indian Doll.
But all she has to do
to love as much
is love the dad who brought her
as much as I loved mine.

No Cuddles, she was lumber stiff,
her limbs incapable of akimbo,
kept ruler straight, like Miss Smith's back,
as admirable stance in a math teacher
that may have been, at school day's end,
a disability in disguise. My doll's
patterned blanket, in primary colors,
was plastered onto her as though she must
fulfill an obligation to attend
some festive, but perpetual Council Fire,
some hell of happiness
that forbids into eternity
a single change of clothes.

I didn't care at all.
In her headband of tiny beads, bright
against the warm red-brown of her face,
and in the geometrics of her blanket
that were like a New World to me,
breaking the monotony of flowers,
she could have been jellyfish, ballerina,
Cuddles herself. Daddy brought her,
to me. Therefore she became

the nearest, dearest of innumerable
bedship companions, every night—
a precious immigrant to Massachusetts
from Moosehead Lake in Maine,
where the forest had no ending,
where the moose and bear were people,
where my father was an Indian.

But then, one night,
my mommy came to tuck me in.
She frowned at Indian Doll, and said,
"What do you like *her* for? She can't
be very cuddly." That wasn't all.
Coiled to spring, she didn't stop
to let me answer, but went on against
my Indian doll, because she was
an Indian! I didn't understand at all,
with love so innocent, so deep,
and I don't know now, but think
an early Oedipal guilt, a sense
I got from my mother then, of more
than just the hate words spewing forth
from all her Puritan ancestors, to 1630,
shamed my defiance into submission.

A night or two later,
or perhaps it was a week,
I wrenched my beloved Indian doll,
most unwillingly, from my Noah's Ark,

my bed. Leaving both of us lonely,
I set her, sadly, on a far white shelf
without even really grasping why.

September 9, 2004

JULY

vapor
blue erasure
how you turn from me
again
to your dreamed daughter
who is only a nurse's aid
but not homely as I am
nor are you
yet I am the mirror
you cannot bear to look at
my face your face
revealing you
naked as indeed you are

I am so afraid
I would like to find you
in pretty juice glasses
more and more
five hundred red roosters
and oranges amidst their leaves
would not be enough imprint
to ease this far watch I keep
over your sure, slow departure
from this earth

as you struggle this week
without me
without anyone
to overcome vodka and vermouth
without me

without anyone
without a glance at the sunshine
falling on the terrace
where two wrought iron chairs
stand empty
without me
without you
without anyone

as if drink were your only problem
as if that long ago day
on the gray downtown street
when you, a child, reached
impulsively to kiss
your mother
and she, Victorian, stiffened
and said no
we never do this in public
she had put a glass of liquor
in your small hand
and left you alone
unable to find your way home

July, 2004

ON OTTER CREEK, AUGUST 17, 2002

On the river this day, flash of awareness
of myself at sixteen, vivid as recall
by smell, as of my chestnut horse's stable;
hay, manure, mustiness combined. Then—
still here on earth at sixty-three,
still alive; in this smooth, shining hide
of summer, its revealing surfaces:
close-fitting coats over muscles
of herons and horses. Its concealing ones:
liquid blacktop of my river road above
a deep cruise of otters, sleek, invisible,
paths crossing under my boat's path;
and green silver of willows hiding,
like a chlorophyll medication,
the autumn in my own blood …

But today, two dark sun horses,
a mare and her own stallion son,
come astonishingly forth
out of the great distance of their pasture
and of loneliness I hadn't known was mine,
or that it was so large, this pleasure day.
I'd felt self-sufficient. Now the sunburst
of these horses reminded me of need
for other beings, and of my gauche shyness
in forming bonds. They came familiarly
to river's edge, to drink. But then,
startled by the stranger, they froze.
I must have been remembering the horse
of my first years, the friends we were,

and I must have seen in these two
his incarnation, to have been so undeterred.
I left my canoe to meet them
where they stood wary, aloof—
I'd almost say mistrustful—at the first
of two low, clay ledges. I began
a foolish one-way conversation to bend
the statues back to life. She was sorrel,
red all over, face refined. But he!

A Belgian workhorse in all but height,
he was huge at fourteen hands, and flaxen;
great rounded rump, neck half the sun,
and a blaze down his Roman face to stamp
his right to kingship, should it come.
I never saw a fellow so surprising, so
in and out of proportion at once, as he.
I'd love to have gentled him, for when
I'd talked to both awhile, I offered grass,
and he came only once to take it, then
stepped back and held his ground, standoffish
for lack of much acquaintance with my kind.

The pretty mare got friendlier, allowing me
to scratch behind her ear, brush dried mud
from her neck, raking with my fingers. This
soon reached a point where she nestled
her warm head, lovingly, against my breast,
as if I were the person she belonged to,
and had been all along; and then she walked
down over both mud banks, curious,
to investigate my boat. She seemed

to scrutinize the space requirements;
tried a bit of the stern seat. Was she
going to eat it out to improve them?
Wide-eyed, I looked on. Suddenly,
she grabbed one of my filthy socks
lying in the bottom of the boat,
and dropped it in the water! I had to admit
they badly needed washing. Now she stood
with head lowered over the gunwale,
and I more surely read her purpose.
Indeed she *had* been doing a thoughtful study.
She was going to step into my green craft
and ride away with me to new, lush pastures
wherever they might be! I would have been
hard taxed to put a stop to this, for I
could see the three of us, I paddling,
the mare riding, her chunky son swimming,
sometimes wading with big, churning strokes,
and the looks on the faces of the couple
I'd earlier passed, if they, kayaking,
should behold this arresting cavalcade
that would include a horse in a canoe!

It was not to be. She may have had
some serious, instinctive doubts about
the horseworthiness of my craft. Twice more
she moved from it to me, to it to me.
At last she bared her teeth to bite my toes,
but this was just more curiosity, unless
it was to prod me to the boat and our adventure?
I hadn't thought of this 'til now. Oh, surely
this was it, and I was blind! But I have not

such acreage as theirs for them, here at home.
Where was I? She missed my toes.

I could have turned then toward the boat,
inviting them to follow. But these beasts
did not, in fact, belong to me, and so
I had to say good bye to them too soon.
It was too abrupt, too absolute!
When I paddled off alone, looking back,
they were rumps to the river, their tails
swishing in unison against the flies.
Oh, horses, I'm sorry!
I'm sorry that the lives we long for
so often seem to be realized
only in such moments, unexpected, brief,
as this of ours. I should've stolen you!
And yet, because of you,
a day of perfect loveliness was given flesh;
my river's spell suffused with lights
charged with earthly tenderness.

March 30, 2004

HIDEOUT

How cowardice loves nonconformity!
It's a guarantee that I will die
in one of the months of the year,
although that's quite conventional,
isn't it? Like everybody else!
A specialist in hiding out,
a moth in a sweater's sleeve,
by rights should find
a space between March and April
that no one knows about,
is not on any calendar; or it is
an eddy's suck in the season's flow
and backflow, but wee, more hidden
than a crevice in a cavern
near the ocean's floor,
still waiting for its first
spiraling, quick worm
after eons of time.

I don't know why I made my will
to land me in Hope Cemetery,
a Manhattan for the dead. Oh,
just everyone is there! Now
I would reject my very parentage,
it seems—that deep a bond—
rather than be moved
(not that they'll find me)
from this slit that widens
in the bottom muck
to receive me,

a vaginal ground entrance
into the womb of lost weathers.
Lying there undisturbed
by the snowmelt water's force,
a poor sopped flutterer
about to enter,
I am listening to my wings
tell me that they will never
stand me up again, nor fly me
back into the leaf dance playhouse
of the weeping willow
in which I've played at being friends,
though no one else was there;
from which I've never dared emerge
into any sort of involvement
in real people's lives.

March 24, 2005

CONFESSIONS OF JONAH'S WIFE

"...and his years were 535, and Jonah did give up
the ghost. But the ghost of Jonah did not give up,
but took unto itself a wife, who was called Ruth,
and they did make their home in the whale where
Jonah had once vacationed three days and nights, and
which he had enjoyed more than he let on to God.
And in the seventh season of spawning there was
merry-making, and to Jonah's ghost in that season a
thing did come to pass..."

>After Jonah died
>I settled down in a new whale,
>with pillow, pots, and pot.
>
>For a while I sighed,
>and thought of mastering some braille,
>But then decided not.
>"After all," I said,
>While scrubbing the intestine floor
>(A rather lengthy task),
>
>"Since the old man's dead
>I ought to have some rest in store,
>So where's that unused flask?"
>
>Then I lit a match—
>A fish half-chewed slid straight on by
>And promptly put it out.
>
>"Nuts to you, damned catch,

I'll smear your carcass smooth on rye,
And butter up your snout."

Nowhere could I find
My balm; then guessed I'd left it—oh,
Oh—in the other whale!
"Jonah wouldn't mind,"
I thought, "how much I need for woe
The lost unHoly Grail."

"In what neighborhood
Might our old home be spouting now?"
I simply couldn't tell.

Thinking if I could,
I'd charm it here if just somehow
I worked a mermaid spell.

I crawled out the back
And held my nose and held my hopes
And said a wriggly prayer.

Lo, I had the knack!
My legs coiled 'round in slimy ropes
Until no longer there.

"God is round-about,"
I cried, and then our house appeared,
And I fell to my fins.

Our chimney did spout,
and my awed vision grew a-bleared

Before our home's huge grins.

Through our door's dear rasp
In sudden ache I heard a cough,
And then I saw two legs.

"Jonah!" I did gasp
And looked again and saw enough;
(His legs are like two kegs).

"Ruth!" my love did say.
"Where have you been, with whom,
    and why?
It has been seven years."   "Yes."
   His voice held sway
Like horrid doom, and made me cry
As in his absent years.

"You must be alive,"
I said when I had found my breath.
"Why didn't you tell me?"

"Ruth, let us strive
To mend this most erroneous death."
He skipped the mystery.

"No, it cannot be.
Alas, I am a mermaid now
And cannot swim with *you.*

"Fish are in the sea
On whom sweet charms I must bestow,
And so, my dear, Adieu."

Undated

THE SHEEP

In treeless Iceland, I watch sheep
make sudden, nervous leaps
above the coast grass and rock,
expressing fear so openly
that I envy them. Not too close,
I still can see it might be ewes
escaping rams' approach. No snakes
on this island. Although it is
so ordinary, these creatures focus
my wonder in a wandering wind.
Shag wool roped, long as Viking hair,
they look as free and wild
as I would like to be.

There must be fences I can't see,
off far enough to let me think
the whole island is their pasture,
and when they fade from view,
moving toward the long horizon
into gray glow that is the color
of this cold land, I notice now
brushy white tufts of cotton grass
flocking in the foreground field.
It is the sheep remembered.

I have hidden in so many ways,
afraid even to be afraid. Penned
tight, I don't know what lies beyond
my self-confinement. I am not
vivid like the sheep, telling all

in each moment. I'm too complex!

On the train ride to Icelandic Air,
the run-on list of common ailments
of the old woman I was trapped beside
for forty eight hours on a coach car,
who forced me into sympathy, to say
"cluck, cluck" with the "clack-clack"
of the wheels, over and over, I went
deaf to, well short of destination.

I'd have liked her with the courage
to transcend! I know that stranger
too well, her face my face,
by telling all, telling nothing much.

Maybe we're all opposite to beasts,
revealing most by leaving out.
But I could use a little more
of their innocence. I anticipate
too well by now the kinds of slights
that will diminish me. I'm too good
a forecaster of weather. Should I be
so sure? The presentness of the sheep
is what I love them for. But,
what in them is so instinctive
in me would be a brave simplicity,
a courage not to hide, but just to be.

I see them still, in wild thyme
in magenta clusters that shiver
with a barely discernible motion

beside their sharp hooves, in wind
that's a song with a waiting form—
my song, that I would sing
with grass, and thyme, and sheep
in Iceland.

January 27, 2005

GOING FROM DOOR TO DOOR

It's the broad waste of midday.
In hope and trepidation, I press
a doorbell's button. If this were night
I would
        listen for footsteps on a floor.
gaining volume 'til they reached the door.
        shift my weight self-consciously
from left to right, in anticipation of
a hall and porch light coming on.
        try to straighten my spinal curvature
a bit, before the door is opened. How?
A tiny, cautious crack or maybe
it'll be flung wide!

But it's the pale expanse of noon hour,
color of sand. I'm aware of that
even in the shelter of these rhododendrons
that bloody the slant marble stoop here
with their red shadow; even though
a miniature, fairy tale forest stretches
no more than twenty yards out,
enclosing, darkening to rich midnight
this quaint old Cape, ink blotter blue,
that looks to me to have sunk
like a fieldstone step
deeper into earth with time.

A rectangular blackness faces me,
thick as lava flow, but nothing of it
moves …unless perhaps the molecules

that, when a child, I used to think
that I could see sometimes, as in
a shaft of light full of dust motes—
little did I know! It is the door,
of course. It may be open now,
it's hard to tell. It may be closed.
Open or closed doesn't matter
if no one is inside.

Oh, why don't you come?
Oh, I know now who you are
I wait for, having trudged so far
through the desert day in which
I ought to be at work, trying amidst
unaccountably ugly surroundings
to play my part, to give something;
not be standing here in this lush,
blue-black oasis brightened only by
a small pool of crimson around my feet.

Oh, why don't you come,
my mother, my self, my wellspring
even when shallow in drought?
Old, small now, and creeping frail,
but you! If this is
really night, the one beyond
proper visiting hours, how will I
ever now
come to believe I have a being
worth offering, as I continue on

a very dusty way, my back to you,
going from door to door?

August 20, 2006

REAL ESTATE NEEDS

Speaking to her of her way
with Amy and Davey
put David and Meg into a fond embrace,
until they remembered
that Davey and Amy were myths
born of their childlessness.

Then, after a week not talking,
the nerves fingernails
on a blackboard of silence,
eyes averted from each other's
timid compulsions to connect,
their new little house on Cape Cod
was smashed by the next door condo
when a sea gale lifted it from its lashings
and, in one great gust,
blew it hard against theirs.

"How little it takes to rock the boat,"
Meg sighed to Dave nonsensically,
from under a double boiler
perched jauntily on her head.
She spoke in a voice of domesticity,
of almost relishing complaint,
in fantasy insensate to the storm,
and then, to keep the sense
her dream life made, she imaged
Davey setting Amy's toy boat,
holding her favorite doll,
loose from its moorings,

Amy swimming out after it,
Amy floundering far from shore,
a lifeguard sent out to rescue her.
After this,
a canceled weekend of picnics and swims,
a daughter's new fear of water.

As her fantasy receded,
it was odd to her how its own pain
seemed a mere curtsey to reality,
that she had inserted dutifully
against the very purpose of such dreaming.

At first, in self-pity,
they retreated to the cellar,
but it felt as claustrophobic there
as it would be to breathe
inside a sleeping bag inside a chimney.
There seemed no point in staying there,
so they squirmed back up through the rubble
and thought about buying an old bungalow
they'd seen across the peninsula—
gray weathered sticks, really, in a bay—
which might beat the flying condos to it,
as it was about to collapse anyway.
Sliding down their kitchen floor
backwards against a remaining wall,
like Chaplin in that glacier cabin,
they mentally clinched the deal.
They both liked the outdoor shower
at the top of rickety outside stairs…
they were forgetting now,

in their confusion,
their longing towards continuance,
towards Amy and Davey.

That would come right back to them
in this next house falling down.
Yet how could it be, after such havoc,
and in a woman so securely locked
behind the door of her suburban dream,
that Meg would miss the Atlantic waves
beyond the saltwater marsh, on open sea?
and wild winds, unimpeded, driving?
She had heard the ocean's everlasting boom,
low, yet often drowning
the sleep growl of their dog in his corner.

Although she didn't see it, or see
that her most compelling daydream wasn't free
unless she could be,
they had composed her most real estate.
How could this go on? But it would.
The ceaseless waves would pull against
her housebound heart like ebb tide
drawing her back. Whisper on the sand
She *heard* in off-guard moments
that awaited only conscious knowing
to release her from a rigid fence
of tulips that was all she could allow
herself of self-expression. And fulfillment
would try, by busy practicality, to forbid
even those isolate, chance instants
of free identification with the wild,

and could disappoint more cruelly still
than the trash left in the storm's wake.
Meg could find a saving grace,
but would it be
the children of her flesh
or just a more attentive listening?

From the open window she had watched
the breakers toss gulls of their flesh
skyward in quick, decisive bursts
and had seen one plummet down,
foam to form to foam. The sea had been
a close reassurance of passion, danger
just past the grasses and dunes
that fenced it from the tranquil marsh,
with its dully floating detritus,
that had mirrored their days.

September 17, 2000
(revised fall/winter 2005/2006)

THE HERMIT SAID

I am reported dead periodically,
about every twenty years, and
each time they almost believe it.
They say, "That's funny, I thought …
but no, I guess it's now."
I know that's how it is because
one time I stood right behind
two people who were talking about me,
and one said to the other,
"Did you read today's gazette?
Crazy June is dead." The other
shrugged, said, "That's funny,
I thought …" and then she
sought another topic, but not without
looking around, as if to make sure;
and saw me standing there.

May 1, 2006

IMMACULATE GLIDE OF SUMMER

Immaculate glide of summer out of time,
I lilt with you and the swan boats
And the softly rushing tree.
Its breath bends over a pond,
Delicate as whispered dread
Of the first red leaf it must let fall.
They are a mother and her clear child,
Who will wither, she knows, sooner than she,
Leaving the shell of her.
A drought of waters sought
Like a touch will bring
Orders of funerals in the fall.

I will bury your cat, O lamplit summer,
And remember skimmed milk or an opal flying,
As if color sponsored every mood I wish to keep.
In murdering the mirrors of creation,
I seek to live again, anew.
Yet my oars have nerves of recollection
Potent as the other faces which,
Reflected in my ponds, believe them.
The iron epitaphs I spell
Are hollow after all.

Will my left hand always rise against
The children who every summer grow
From the left of my heart's land?
I prepare the alphabet of their names
That my hungry hand will trace,
And I will hear the ring of echoes

And faint gospels golden as tombs.
While through summer's gossamer tent
I will see the colors of clothes
Carry real worlds and bright silence.

Undated

MEADOW'S CHILD

I still insist on paradise.
I am the child my parents left alone
at a cabin door, watching
that empty field fill with fireflies.

Old Chuck Wood, who eats my garden,
curls in a favored chamber underground.
It could be my own left ventricle.
I am too tempted toward pardon.

Stars so very distant, they could die
before we see their light, came close
my eighth summer, as black-eyed susans,
fireflies. These were eternity.

In child's time, looking neither back
nor forward, such arrest is possible.
But now, unable ever to forget her
as she was, so happy in her lack

of complications, my old heart tries
to hold time still, as if by facing loss
I would lose her. All my life's lasting
I owe the child and her fireflies.

But it's a perilous path to stretch
a moment's bliss beyond itself, and I
have failed so much to try it.
And now, tonight, if I could catch
a firefly on the wing, and see it still

to rest upon my palm, parallel lines
of folded wings opening to greengold
flares in the velvet dark until

a bat, perhaps, threatens or there comes
a cooling of my sleepy hand that sends it
like a shooting star away, and traffic
through the imprisoning city hums
like chronic and incurable pain
in my imagination, I could almost
let it go if I could hope to win
respect, friendship, love. Oh, when

did I split, self from self, forbidding
maturation? Oh, meadow's child!
By innocence you're held in simple light.
Blind, brutal world! How? What wedding?

July 28, 2005
Revision: August 10, 2007

SAID POND

Was it so named by the first comers,
or they who thought they were?
Or am I pronouncing it wrong?
Does it rhyme with "aid" or "Ma Mead,"
the way an Arabian might say it?
Though mapped, and visited now and then,
the path here disappears in spots,
and I have come here
this fair late summer morning
so lonely, so alone
that its present perfect isolation—
its barely rippled surface
broken soundlessly by three ducks;
its bordering goldenrod
in bright, noiseless September bloom;
its fishes making their small
silver splash, scarcely heard—
is almost more than I can bear.

I want to swim, the water's deep,
and it's ninety-plus degrees today,
but the place is sacrosanct, too still:
it belongs to beavers, now lodged in sleep.
But this mottled toad
who moves toward me
rather than away,
pale throat pumping,
who freezes by my left foot,

more as if seeking another body
than in an effort to camouflage…
is he, so much a part
of this wordless, choiceless landscape,
also more? Is he lonely, too?
Is he, then, in some sense, aware?

But I mean
what if, deep-down, I have no language?
What if, like the oval yellow leaf
that's just butterflied onto a spider web
and caught there vertically
in mid-air, I *am* this place?
Unable to explain. Unspoken for.

If lonely is, in cosmic terms,
all each of us is or can be,
and it's said to me here
beyond all human, loud disruptions
that try so hard to silence Silence—
here where red dragonflies,
pinships molten in the sun
and drawn to be as if I were an island,
take in the air that I breathe out;
the marsh-harbored sora calls twice,
but not again:
and a great blue heron lifts and sails—
I do recall other days
when such a setting meant to me
only simple peace; and I think

some courage for the human world,
although it's given me great pain,
could help me
so to remember this one,
for both are my relations
and each will call and call.

September 6, 2010

THE BLACKSTONE: A DIARY

Through our city
the river ran mostly underground.
But there was a place,
my father knew of it,
where it briefly surfaced.
One day we went there, just to see.
I was very young. I remember
a dense black flow, and a daytime dark
around me where I stood
between them, father and mother,
who were to me,
in that small black grove,
two tall trees.

Whatever age you have to be
to conceive of this
I must have reached, for I saw
The river leading to some future;
and then, with an intuition
very quiet, very sure
I knew my mother would die.

Why not both?
As fate had it, my father then
had less than ten more years
and my mother, over sixty.
I liked my father better
and I loved him
as father and mother both—
my favorite dolls were animals!

So it wasn't that he figured less.
Why not both? I don't know.
It only came to me that she would go.
It was about her.
And, rather than a new recognition
of a fact applicable to all,
as it surely must have been,
I've recalled it always
as a psychic's uncanny augury, almost;
not that I could've said
the how and where and when.

Every night of my childhood
Red Riding Hood, my dollhouse doll,
mother of the household,
fell through the earth
in an elevator shaft
without an elevator.
Down and down and down and down
she dropped, until I was asleep,
immortal Bow Wow in my arms.

Two tall trees, but one
was galled by lack of self-esteem,
so there was not much teaching
not doing things together;
there was a great space between us
like the field across the street;
and the sense of it inside me
widened, lengthened the field.
On the scale of human failings,
this seems so very common,

so well-known, even influential
toward some good as well as ill:
the field, in mist, a haunting loveliness
to turn to time and time again,
until my turning away
from her turning away
became a turning to
for open country's own sake.
Still, I kept on looking for her
in the sofa's summer slipcover's
large yellow flowers,
in the purple and yellow backyard
pansies bordering the house,
in the soft purple lilac hedge
dividing yards…
anywhere but where she was,
for no one knew where that was,
especially not the needing child.

No one knew where I was
through her long last years
when I sought out bobolink meadows,
several in the county,
to escape the house,
to escape her,
to escape myself,
to make, for a few permissible hours,
our visits more bearable.
I would see them burst,
in colors of coal and milk and sun,
up from their grass-hid nests
to their helicopter hesitations

to pour the reverse waterfalls
of their bubbling song back down
to the listening young.

She sounded like a bobolink
in her sudden rush of words—
so very long repressed
in normal social scenes,
and from me, and even from
a genuine friend, I think—
to her Paid Help,
a woman she believed in
for nineteen years, who posed
as her nurse's aide, and who,
entrusted with her bank books,
began to rob her blind;
planned a kidnap
to her own home
that would have ended
when the money did;
and in discard
of the body, still alive,
to the worst of nursing homes.

She nearly got away with it.
But now I run ahead a bit
to say my mother saved herself
with a call to the family lawyer,
who was an honest friend,
begging him to get her out
of a place she was put in
and she did die in her own bed.

(Because she walked
away from me too much
throughout our lives
her actual death
seemed a subtle, further step
into another room,
when it came. But why hers,
not his? Of course it was,
I see this now,
the enormity of her mattering to me,
somehow magnified
by her lifelong means of absence.

And yet I also know
there is another story
waiting not too patiently
that finds a moment
in which she quietly
and very gently rescued me,
with a few right words,
from a thing
that could not be borne.)

Two months before my mother
went away for good,
having become dangerously ill,
I, still as blind to wrong
as she, from need,
daily drove to see her
in an intensive care home
in the imposter's outlying town
Initially unexpected,

it was intended as a way station
before the aforementioned move.

On the way there,
from the unfamiliar city street
I took to reach the highway,
I'd catch a glimpse of the Blackstone—
that river I'd never happened upon
nor had ever tried again to find
between that distant day of prophesy
and this, its fulfillment—
on my left. In Whitinsville, I know,
it travels no more as a portent
in the half-forgotten, back recesses
of the mind. Just as the evils
any of us may succumb to
if not always pre-plotted
and so brazen as this,
have a way of coming
finally to light,
it runs no longer underground.

June 4, 2010

UNICORN FIELD

Almost invisible in a circle
of bent, yellowed, frosted blades
surrounded by grass that kept
somewhat more of its summer green
and less of winter's brittling,
the circle a filled-in halo
at the dark of the moon that said
this couldn't be moonlight,
at the deep end of dusk that said
skylight where the sun had been
could only show it, not be it,
the unicorn stood
no larger than a pony
and very finely boned,
a white whisper, a frozen breath,
a wish that ran from my halter
and stopped in its own
pale, mysterious glow;
and one sharp, black, raised hoof
gave a cocky stamp
down onto the crunchy, rooted hay.
As I walked nearer, I saw
that it then held its stance,
proud in its perfection,
too safe in its illusory nature
to fear I could ever rein it back,
ever harness it to what is real.

December 2, 2010

WHEN THE FOREST WALKS

A bear!
In the dusk woods that skirt my camp.
The trunks of his legs
are four trees walking.
I start to image this fear that grows
for my dog, and for both of us
because of her—she could provoke
an attack!—and I see
four more trunks move, four more,
until a whole dim battalion
begins its march to the water,
the water of our hidden cove.
I can't just stand, silent watcher.
Yet we are not quite in his path,
she and I; I'm not actually overcome
as I turn to her; but I'm uncertain
what to do! Just leash her?
Asleep on the pine duff, she wakes
to the rank scent and instantly *knows*,
without foreknowledge. She knows
this great presence may swerve.
Before I can take a single step
she streaks to our small tent,
to me, an illusion! I think,
because our bond is as mother/child,
that she believes in it
as she believes me, dear soul,
that I will always save us, that
our tent, my weak provision, to her
is foolproof as she must feel

my love for her to be.
But something I won't hear now speaks.
It says, No. She's unerring instinct now,
acting independently to save herself
as, in a pinch, *I might, too,*
and this is it—is it all?—
just get out of sight!
I cannot be so simple, so simply smart.
But, imagining claws tear at cloth, at skin,
I follow her in, too stupid
not to need *her* to guide *me*;
and I lie down there with her
in the shelterless world,
on this earth bed that has so often
comforted, confused to learn our separateness—
oh, doubting our strong attachment!
As the surging ursine shapes become
mere trees again, and the bear becomes
a passerby, can I trust again
what is my deepest need to know—
that we are home, on the wild earth
and for each other?

April 26, 2003
(revision of last 6 lines: 3/20/10)

WISH LIST

Dear Mother

I want a whale for Christmas.

If you knew what I mean,
that would be the end of this poem.

But I don't think you do know,
so perhaps I'd better tell you.

I don't want this white convertible
with blue upholstery and fins

that could make me popular,
you prayed, at school.

I don't want this ball gown
in layered, sea green chiffon.

This year, I want a blue whale.
I'll call him Blue Louie.

I'll call him that,
but I won't keep him long.

I just want his eye, directed by
a brain as large as his must be

to look into mine for an instant
to feel what might transpire.

Now do you understand me? No?
and then I want his many yards

to glide away, and blend
into the only world he knows.

What is it you think of me
beneath what you want me to be?

Do you even like yourself? Or me?
What are these things and things

you shower in breaking waves
over my misshapen skull?

Mother, if I could find a love to keep,
it would be where you cannot find me.

Somewhere along an ocean trail,
when I've been snorkeling too long,

I'll turn into a blue whale.
Through underwater canyons,

Park Avenues of the sea, myriad
bright shapes will swim in unison

all the time, except to rest,
noses to crevice walls,

tails outhanging;
and when I find him, if I do,

Love will ask no questions,
none such as I ask you;

nor any answers. He and I
will cruise without a conscience

or a dream. We are the dream,
moving weightless, blue in blue...

> Here her mother,
> unable to help or hope,
> bursts
> into unstoppable tears.

September 11, 2010

ALSO RAN: THE TRUTH

Paddling off in my boat so mainly
I guess I've practiced deceit so long
that it seems like The Way.
So I may not have a poem here
with The Way so deeply troughed
that all I see is tips of silos
over the mud bank of it,
the honesty of conflict looking like
The Criminal. Oh, I always fail
when the title comes first,
sitting like the mayoress of Notown
surprised in her conceit
by the nonexistence of her citizens.
The farmer's cities of corn
can make or break him, of course,
Those yellow-toothed folk stay real
while I, from the stern seat,
look up at the skywriting:
ALSO RAN: THE TRUTH
in its dissipating white trails,
its vanishing letter-tails.

November 8, 2011

HALF A PRAYER, VERSION 2

My limbs resigned in cherry sleep
I strangle with the miser in his orchard;
The shears of his habit stuck in my throat,
I cling to his lapels, and watch him close;
So with my eyes, in pallid green a-fawning,
I caress the lowly doctor,
And prune the laws that knell provisionals,
A hundred crusty bells hollow
In the hanging gardens of his heart.

Deep in the yearnings of day's poor second,
Sly as a cat I beacon yellow through a rock;
My secret bounces from the one beyond
Like a whisper grained with age;
Bleeding in the lungs I follow
The chinking of the goodman bells;
And gardener and minister he hauls me
By my pupils to the pulpit and the greensward soft,
Where I rest like the hull of the holy vessel;
My secret leaks through the bottom of the cup.
All over his cherubic red reality I rain
Until he drowns in the hour of his downpour,
Done straining amid clusters of the emblem.
Look, I cry, as we grope in the orchard
Of the lost islands,
And I snip an Easter lily stem:
No blood trembles in the chalice of a flower.

Leeward of my age the eggs and rabbits
Huddle and crack on the deck that does not wreck

Unless, when child flowers from child,
I pluck my holidays from the money-tree
and close the portholes of my eyes
That once were pollen-glazed,
Where I swam upright in a sun-filled pond,
And saw a lawn of the lake sprout supple waves
To bend in the easy tidings of sunday;
Though this abortion leave life weeping
I will not waken to the churchgate toll,
But cherry-ripe keep slumber in the grey cocoon
And lure and lesson like the sweet green troll
Dancing through a rinse of gleams,
Deaf confessionals in the crooked festival.

Undated

ANTITHESIS
(while descending Shrewsbury Mountain)

Coming back down,
balsam to balsam and birch
to birch and beech to beech,
my old bones shout like fractures
at the joints. The mountain's
evil spirit, feeling playful,
is piercing with a cattle prod
to hips, knees, shoulders, neck.
The good spirits are in their den,
playing poker. Until one looks up,
hearing misery. Mine. He arranges
a meeting. The slug and I don't
make eye contact, don't
exchange any words, but
when my pain points meet his lounge
upon a boulder, he could be
live bandaid on rock scratch
except the squish of him that is he
stretches out on a moist moss bed
oh so deep, so deep,
in a cool splay of bliss. He says
to my bones grating on bones,
"Pleasure has no joints, you know,
happiness needs no face, and,
whereas warmth can lead to rashes,
watery plush is yes, is yes
is sleep without dream's shake-up
is dream too sweet for need of sleep
is yes, just this, yummmm…"

and my bones begin to dissolve,
pills in water, watching him,
his orange slime aglitter
with countless tiny dots
in the forest-gentled light…
the striking antithesis
of this slug and this me
surely pertains beyond
trials merely physical. And,
as I was about to say,

his emanation of utter peace
within a perfect sense of place
upon this mountain works
as antidote to my hurts,
inspires empathic identification
until I, too, am almost slug.
Slug of Shrewsbury.

August 3, 2011

BESIDE THE MILLHOUSE

For almost a whole year now
I've lived with the realization
that my cousin's coffee mug, the one
flowered pink and blue that says
"Always your mother, Now your friend"—
and the way she handed it to me
twice or maybe three times,
the same one, not some other,
describes our relationship
according to her. I have been
too deeply offended, to mortified
to want to write, call, or see her
and when I've done so
it hasn't been the same as before,
as when I held the illusion or
delusion? that we are equals.
For almost a year now
I have just hated her.

It's nearly two months since the floods.
Yesterday I decided, after my appointment
to oil undercoat my car, to check out
the two local covered bridges,
see how they fared. The first, and nearest,
was defiled by graffiti two months
before the torrent broke apart the road,
left its cemented stone foundation hanging
out beyond the boulder it sits upon.
JUNE 30, 2011 THUG LIFE CHRISTINA
scrawled hugely throughout the dark interior

over and over, end to end. Oh, loneliness.
The second bridge, next town over, mostly
looked all right. Just upriver from it
is where my cousin lived in 1968.
A yellow farmhouse; a grist mill
downbank by the river; a barn.
She, her husband, and six kids of eight
still at home. The house held them all,
and some lost souls, of whom I was one.

An elder music teacher recovering
from yet another heart attack;
a youth whose family home
was two crossed boards in a woods;
an alcoholic me, and a schizophrenic
friend of mine. The floorboards groaned.

Yesterday a small sign invited me
into an enclosure housing prints
and notecards of the bridge and mill.

The millhouse is an apartment now,
and there's an artist living there.
So I found myself on a post-flood rock wall
near ground I hadn't touched since '69.
I looked down at the roily river
remembering the rocks, the waterfalls,
and trying to recall where we swam
one day, a few of the kids and I.
I thought I might purchase
a box of the notecards, to send one
to my cousin, a pleasing reminder

of her one-time home. Send kids some, too,
But then I felt,
still looking down at time and the river
from the smooth new wall,
how I may not know my cousin anymore;
and my sense of this was free
of the moral self-examination and judgment
that should've been there
in my consciousness; I only felt,
as if there were justification,
how a long, long chapter
that for forty two years I assumed
would read on until there was a death,
may possibly have closed without one.

October 27, 2011

HOPE

I'm weeding clumps of long grass
        from the corners
of my burning, dirt-scratched eyes.
        I'm dreaming
from this brown, stony underworld of
        resurrection
on a mirror lake, a second birth
        at six a.m.,
three hours sooner than the first,
        so as not
to be right on time for dulling work,
        but for a shaft
of sunlight. It will be a birth
        that glides
like my old, beat up, loved canoe
        just paddled
into the yellow strait of devotion.

June 6, 2011

ROAD WALK

I imagine the gunshots,
muffled by distance,
are little burst puffballs
as heard by insects.
"Poom, poom, poom."
Perhaps the tan moth,
life-light in its wings
calling its bluff
as dead leaf piece scattering,
can detect the soft explosions
flying low, as it does,
and near enough to disappear
in a smoky brown cloud,
a dollhouse chimney fire.
I'm running from my fear again,
which is not of where I am,
but if gunfire is its metaphor
I have it, by escaping,
downsized to a diorama.

Liar!
I won't realize the silence
of these November woods
either side the road I walk
is shrill with trepidation:
the terror of the deer.
I only love the dark light
and its quiet mystery
that I won't try to name.
Oh, I love it so.

The deer are not there.
Once this stillness spoke
their suspense to me.

You see, I felt this morning
a relinquishing, as if
I might like to die now.
But I put on blaze orange,
cap and vest,
in case I'd rather put it off,

and *then* I went out to the hunt,
only as a walker,
keeping to the road.
Shots are coming in closer,
but it's not Afghanistan.
I'm not the target.
Adolescent farce!
Am I so in love
with my own victimhood
that I can so forget
another's pain?
No longer identify?
Oh, and this cowardice
that I even disown my own!

Beside the road now
bloody ribcage segments
rise in three arcs
with blunt-end toothy crossbars,
short and curved,
a macabre sky-eating sculpture.

The hide, with taupe fur,
skillfully stripped off
in one whole piece,
is draped over the remains
like a thrown-off blanket,
as if the poor beast's soul
had just got out of bed
to start its journey.

I remember now
the young buck in Maine,
the flash of astonishment
that held in his summer face,
red squirrel orange
raised a tone or two,
as we froze in close encounter
across a path. The questioning way
he cocked his head, I could tell
that I was the very first
human being he'd ever seen.
"Who *are* you?"
Enormous, his eyes,
their brown lights startled.

All the forest's secrets
could one day lodge in them,
opened, altering his expression
right down to the black nose.
Still antlerless in July,
but a stature almost horse high,
he was so beautiful,
his innocence so large

a thousand miles of safe zone
could not have encompassed it.
It made us equals in surprise.
It made a fellowship of two
joined in wonder. It seemed
to take me back into my own.
Yet I had to know better.
So I hoped. I hoped
so hard for him to live
at least a little while:
another summer, and another,
against the vicious odds.
I hoped so hard.

November 22, 2011

THE OLD WOMAN CRIES...

Homely I was,
homelier I became
and that is why
last night I imagined
my breasts were bobolinks!
On the practical side,
I did think of the holes
I'd have in my tees
and other tops where
the beaks would poke through.
Still, a couple of bobolinks
would be pleasing breasts to have
in their tri-colors
of coal and milk and sun...
especially when they'd sing!
I think I'd go topless
        all summer.

December 20, 2011

WHO AM I?

A mouse has curled
much as if asleep,
or awake and needy,
childlike,
in one of my boot prints
along the home trail.
Its posture speaks
the life that was.

Fur winter gray, dainty legs
frozen pink, in shades
too loud, like some
translucent bubblegum:
thick, but stretched
over the long white bone
Belly round, full of young.
Nose intucked, held in forepaws,
its final protective gesture.

This heart of mine
does not surprise me
with its sentimental lie—
that feels as if the mouse
had known me to be loving
and, cold and hungry,
had sought me out
in the nearest thing
it could find of me,
my footstep in the snow.

I know, of course, that Mouse
saw in that depression only
 a shallow windbreak, no more—
and that more complex seeker
is only me in mouse clothes,
crying for myself
in my loneliness.

Oh, but there is something else
that takes me always by surprise.
Who am I, what
helpless employee of nature,
who has this burn to save
yet in another hour or week
will wash, bait, set
six traps, and place them
in the most likely corners?

December 14, 2011

A DREAM IN DECEMBER

I'd like to know
how it would feel to ski
over a black bear as he
is about to enter long sleep
just under the mound of snow
his body makes, and I
lifting with his breathing in
sinking with his breathing out…
the oneness I might sense
with everything alive
in the sole, brief moment
of so smooth a ride!

But the shock of having touched
something vulnerable
might very quickly send me
into terrifying doubt.
Will he rise to attack?
Will he shower snow in clouds
as the dark mountain of his being
looms over me in storm?

Caught in a forest opening
within a broken, circling wall
of hemlock, spruce, and pine
far, oh far from anyone
who wears a human face,
I'd have no time
to register confusion, to ask,
like an injured fiance,

who or what it was
in wild harmony's name
I'd thought to join
there beneath December's
"long night" moon.

January 1, 2012

A LASTING IMAGE OF EARS, VERSION 2

From my vantage point
on the high road I walked
above fenced plots of pasture
where the mild green river runs,
I thought the donkey, still housed
warmly in his winter coat, had
a couple of feet of ears,
and when he swung one around
about-faced it, nimble as owl,
to locate, to psyche out me…

well, there were several donks
and each one dish-nosed, sweet.
They stood in a loose cluster
on flattened, unpalatable grass
in the listless pasture
of early, waiting spring.
But when he did that, when he
flipped that monumental paddle
back, to hear the difference
in the soundworks
of my big and little toes,
I acquired
an imaginary station wagon
and drove him
over the dream ruts
straight into my green grass heart.

January 7, 2012

AUGUST AGAIN

A cicada. It comes to me
that this is Mother's birthday month,
for which she spoke
her near-to-last words:
"hot, humid days…"
her voice still clear, a wistful girl's.
Snow fell softly without,
Then, some moments before Danielle
the attending nurse's aid
who replaced the one of nineteen years
who stole her money and had planned
a kidnap to her own home for more—
Danielle, who supervised this dying
something like a conductor
with a goddamned baton—
before she sent me from the room,
I heard, "I hurt!"
cried in that same girl's voice
(although she was ninety now)
to God, perhaps, believing
that it was really true
that no one else was listening.
"I hurt!" Oh, I knew it,
although I had a little fight
within myself to keep
from being that child
of her defining doubt, obedient only
to what she seemed to think of me.
I reached out to smooth her hair,
my own so much the same.

"Don't touch me!" came forth
in that voice so young,
as I quickly withdrew my hand.

August 9, 2012 (revision: 8/15)

ROUND IN SUMMER'S EYE

Through the dreaming poplars
I can see the door swung open,
The doorstep tilting and the door
Suspended in a listless welcome,
As if the moment of a sudden joyous opening
Had been as quickly forgotten;
As if the still, hot day
Had absorbed all memory and reason
Of the people gathered inside,
And nothing remained except passive summer,
Not even a season but a time,
Brooding with suppressed life.

The house lies slanting in the shade;
Hides, a detective off-duty,
Waiting from habit, desiring no one.
I'm ten years old.
I walk a path in dry grasses,
Sun-yellowed, firmed and yet half dreamed
By the sun; half trampled as if
By a distant, kingly decree of the sun.
The afternoon is the limitless sky;
Its bright blue stops me in my tracks
Like a police arrest.
A single cloud passes over the house,
Deepening its natural, unpainted darkness;
It buries my suspicion,
Altering its focus from house to sky.
Instantly I know,
As I stand caught on this gentle crest of summer,

The softly leaning grasses brittling in a flash
From a total lack of breath—
I know, in a second's arousal, too brief for tears,
Agonizing, that this child I've been
Is not growing, cannot grow;
That it must die instead.

The house, a malicious innocent,
Is tucked into a decrepit sleep.
I watch it doze, coiled without muscle,
Below my light windless trail,
And the leaves of the poplars rustle a little,
Starched clothing of a stern father,
A darkly dressed undertaker of a man,
A protector without eyes.
It has no dream
The door hangs open,
An old, unconscious mouth.
From the living room
The cold air drools,
I am shut into the unbelievable Light
Of the first, only sun in its dying;
Its hand clutches me and stiffens.

Undated

"IN THE GRATZEL STORE, INCOHERENT IN ITS GRASP FOR GREED"

With that title, unconsciousness
bows and leaves the stage.
I would so much rather
hire back the handyman I had
than purchase one of those machines
that trim edges
with earsplitting grate and grind.
Definition of "gratzel": 1. Shredded grass.
2. The worst sort of auditory experience of grass.
I would rather, if it weren't
for how acutely he reminded me
of the husband and partner
in homesteading that I never had.

But, come to think of it,
the chances are good that,
even if I'd had a crack
at marrying anyone,
he would've happened to be
about as handy as
a brook trout with a typewriter.
Oh, see him slide o'er every key,
grazing a s d f l k j
lightly as a lover does in foreplay,
but printing not a letter!

3. Gratzel: Disharmony. 3a. Subservience to Greed in lieu
of true satisfactions. 3b. A serious disagreement with

REALITY.

Oh, that's it, all right. That all-hallowed word that stinks.
The angel who pissed her pants.

March 10, 2012

SIGHTING: AFTER AN OLD FRIEND'S DEATH

Fox fire!
in a splash of sunlight
crosses my trail
and I watch him
flicker past dark trunks,
a bit of brush fire escapee,
but more intent than erratic;
the white plume of his tail
floats. It's simultaneous
perceptions here, something uninterrupted
through brokenness. He's propelled
by the usual bite of hunger,
nose closely prowling earth.
The flicker fades as he backtracks,
the way a fox will do,
and then he's gone,
I don't know how,
maybe just topography, an easy dip
into the obscurity he calls home.
Or maybe it was a density
of the greenglowing leaves
that cradled him in
with their quilting.
Had he seen me? I don't think so.

Oh, lest I forget,
back in *my* civilization
of comforts and suffocation
where instincts blur: I am he,
hunter and hunted, sometimes

winning my chances unaware,
hidden unknowing in a September
sanctum of hobblebush
turned burgundy around its green veins,
my one life extended in a tangle
for such colors, such designs!
by a very slight depression
in the forest ground.

September 13, 2012

THE ROAD BACK

I'm in up to my neck,
my feet touch bottom muck
and spring me from snails
as big as pool balls.
I walk and walk through water.
I go the length of the lake,
in boundary-less black;
many fireflies my only markers.
They seem flickering ornaments
in imaginary hedges,
long border walls of lights.
And when I reach the lake's end
and cross the familiar causeway,
I enter blackness total: the forest.
The intelligence in my toes
is all I have to guide me now.
Fat antennae, they sense and sense.
I'm as surprised as blind. I'd thought
that I could not negotiate the dark.
On and on I go until
dawn shows me the road back
to where I started from.

And there
a pale ghost bird raises its wings
and sails toward me, and toward
the morning's first, sturdy toad.
The bird just skims brown pine duff.
It's like an old dream I had of flying,
gull-white so blurred into dim dawn light,

so uncertain
as to be perhaps an apparition.
When I had that dream, I was a child,
waking unsure whether or not
I'd really left the ground.

But waking further, I heard the voice
of a robin on his high wire
sing his here, his now—and mine—
with such assurance and aplomb
it could've been Earth's first day.

July 16, 2012

VISITING

There's a part of me
a small part, surely,
but a part
that just cooperates with time,
goes along, like an obliging friend
invited for a sunday drive.
The summer after Mother died,
on a sunny morning off
from packing up her things,
I went out to the cemetery,
I sat on a curved stone bench,
an arm of the gravehouse
of my maternal great grandparents
and my great, great aunt.
One plot down from my father's
across the paved way from where I sat,
from one of the small and many trees
that pose on slopes and flat terrain
of this vast plantation of progenitors,
the copy talk and squeak note
of a mocking bird. Its progeny, I hoped,
would practice their mimicry so near
where my ashes will lie in their urn.
It was all so matter of fact.
My cell phone rang—my cousin's wife,
nothing special. "Oh, I'm communing
with my ancestors," I explained.
And, really, they could've been alive,
so unemotional it was. A social call
on a still morning, full summer

arrived, take or leave its gifts,
all I'll find. It's late June. Even
the failure of my life, all of it—
its freight train of grief
couldn't crash into this peace I felt,
couldn't spoil the reassuring knowledge
that a mockingbird
will likely sing above my grave.

November 7, 2012

A SWIMMING HOLE WOULD BE NICE

A little swimming hole,
just a little one
on my very own acres
would be so nice.

Lacking it,
and with myriad other small wishes
unfulfilled,
I took a walk

and then an off-trail wander
and came
to a perfect dry ground nest of leaves
held in a spruce roots' arms.

Within it,
four naked ruffed grouse chicks
swam around and around and around,
eager to explore—

long necks outstretched,
chin contacts propelling them forward—
the dizzying , hustling whirlpool
of their just-hatched lives.

June 25, 2013

AS BIRDS ARE WORDS FOR WATER

Water notes of house wren, rose-breasted, wood thrush
      and bobolink beyond upmeadow
and all the overflow waters chiming,
spring's foot on the sustaining pedal…
      the brook songs of the birds
      rise and fall from source to sea
and a hairy woodpecker wrecks the time
      with his sturdy black baton
beating a crazed cacophony on a metal sign.
Laughing with the guy who shoves me off, he,
      the astounding volume
            its brazen echoes
send me on my paddling river way.

Then, as if there were a built-in need
amidst the miles and miles of music
to remind the ear and eye of endings,
beneath a low-lying cloud I see
      a black duck—countering—
          lift, lift, vanish
          quicker than a door shuts
          into his house of sky.

Lost so gladly
on the infant, whichways, sometimes streams
crossing gravel road, filling forest;
in the small, bright lives that find,
in such a maze, their nesting avenues
and dot the over-reaching alders

with primary colors…in this May flood,
    how can I not find a boldness
    not often mine, to embrace it all?
Simply to seek some words for water
    which is life
    as birds are words for water
and not always depend for effect or self-warning
    on disappearances.
        I am a bird.
        I have no foresight.
        I am water.

July 7, 2013

THE BLUE RIBBON

Let the long blue ribbon fly
From the child's hair into tomorrow,
Swift as a lightyear from time past;
It is a dream cut from the sky,
And I wear it still as I travel
The colorless path its cutting left.
A dream so Prussian deep
Waves its consequences, reminding.

And that for which I most yearn
Is the first young sight of it
Back in place, before I came
With the scissors of my desperation.
Memory of the lost doll, a she
Whom I cradled, who wore a blue ribbon.
That was reality, before the shears
Cut and fell from my grasp.
But it was long ago; that reality
Has worn away into the dream;
A dream most real, an invalid queen;
Her weak breath catches at every pain.

What keenest of all my experiences
Led me to the cutting of the ribbon?
What vivid flaw pushed me outdoors
To see the sky, an elsewhere,
Mysterious and blue?
It left my life homely as air
Beyond gravity, without texture;
Now my preference is for a blue ribbon,

And the aging dream of its origin,
Guiding my eyes toward a weightless future,
While the ribbon streams from my hair,
Behind me.

Undated

FERN

Beside a woodland path near water
a group of ferns,
all of them unmoving, save one.
And this was waving wildly
as in a dance;
twisting, circling around itself
with such a seeming independent will,
it might have been human.
As I stood watching this expression
of an overweening wish to live,
I felt, without a word in my head,
that I understood it well.

But then, a darker sense of it
came over me, and I bent to quiet it.
I grasped with forefinger and thumb
the very base of its stem,
where my fingers touched the earth.
It stilled, joining its fellows,
and that's when it occurred to me
that some hidden creature
may have known the threat of my hand
and briefly stopped its severing
of the fern's helpless stem,
foregoing its tasty meal
as it burst, in utter silence, my dream
of what the fern had said to me.
If this idea was true,
then meal and sweet delusion both,
in this world so hard to bear,

were lost only for a time.

If wrong? Not all is sorrow!
It was later, in a field guide,
that I read how the marsh fern
"produces new leaves all summer.
Uncoiling fronds mingle with the others,
which turn and twist with the sun
and wave with the breeze, often forming
a dancing mass of fernery."

So. I should've let nature be!
Despite my strong affinity
I might've been too much put off,
as people are by loners,
and thought that things weren't right
because, of all that flock,
only the one would dance.

September 10, 2013

The quoted lines are by Boughton Cobb, from Peterson's field guide series on ferns. J.S.

FLOWER LESSON

When I think, as I sometimes do,
of the flower no one ever sees,
a blind gentian by a vernal pool,
a herb-robert mid-ledge,
each living out its whole life cycle
without anyone to admire it,
no one capable of doing so
even once happening by;
this thought alone has all
the difference in it that I crave,
and consolation, brief reprieve
from my vanity and its hurts.

Just to see, in my mind's eye,
a bird-planted whim of blue asters
half-hidden in the tall grass
at the rear left corner
of the collapsed house
that no one visits, and wake
from forlorn pathos to realize
that, if they speak loneliness to me,
they are not themselves lonely.

Just this sudden new awareness
will make me smile
and stand a bit more bravely
on my crooked stem.

March 6, 2013

FOR NOW

In the wintry chill, the Snow Dog's breath.
On my cheek, almost a sweetness.
The sun christens each snow crystal:
Emerald, Amber, Ruby, Blue Sky…

This day is the white dog's bark
and I am glad inside it.
It makes no noise
It's only the cold sounding.

If I should lose the image
of the dog, and find no one,
but only the cold sounding.
I'll know wordlessness and dread…

Oh! A little ermine's head pops up
into a hole he's made in the whiteness
at the woodyard's edge. A shape of snow,
but warm, to see myself in.

It's he, the very one, who found
his way into my living room last fall
and danced around the rocking chair
on wee feet. Those feet touched floor

lightly as if a spinner's rolag dropped.
But flesh it, he's a white sausage!—
narrow, long, tubular. He made an outline
of arcs, a slinky bounding stairless.

Two stationary trains
closely side by side. When
the other moves, vibration makes you
sure the moving train is yours.

I could only watch in wonder.
Taut, lithe, rippling with surprise
to be inside a human's house.
It was I who danced!

Today his pebble eyes, so black
I can only guess their lights,
see me, and in the fear
that properly belongs to wild things,
he disappears, becomes again snow.
"So, Beauty. You're still here,"
I say to the silence. Its totality
includes now a tiny respiration.

So slight a thing can almost save.
My walk a bright passage, dark surrounding,
the ermine stops me at its exit
and, like a safe lock, keeps it.

He is, for now, that other being
or beings, that presence
without whom
even memory melts away.

January 30-March 20, 2013

FORECAST

I love and love the cold wind
that picks the roof snow up
and swirls it in a cloud.
I love the isolation of it
that envelops me. I love
my loneliness. I forget
the many fears that accompanied
the desire that moved me
to this place I could die in,
the winter's white hospital,
before I even realize
where else and how I also
might have lived, who loved.

March 6, 2013

HEDDI

Class divisions build a fence
of seeming safety around my home,
in the face of a larger world
full of evils; the separation
between my garden and the street
grows an attitude
that leaves no room to notice
the evil *it* is,
here in this smaller room
of polished furniture and silver
where it sidles to a rest,
a misshapen flower of light
upon a knob of table leg
that eerily glows.

A child in idle time,
I sit on the floor
to play the spokes
of my upended Schwinn bicycle
as if it were a harp,
while aging Heddi tries,
in the quick intakes of air
her chronic shortness of breath permits,
to harbor enough O_2
to finish cleaning this dining room,
chore on which her life depends.

I am nine or ten years old.
Suddenly she turns to me
to tell me I am lucky

that I'll never have to do
what she does for a living.
This is a brand new concept
I couldn't have imagined,
there on my music island.
Her soft voice sounds hard.

A new stranger,
a ghost become a person,
helplessly I watch her leave
the comforting family constellation
my innocence had made her
such a simple part of:
Heddi, always there on fridays
when I came home at one from school.
"Di dee di dee di," she sang
over and over,
every friday afternoon,
to the rhythm of her rag.

November 11, 2013

HUNTING SEASON AND A MEETING REMEMBERED

The silence
of these November woods
is shrill with trepidation;
the terror of the deer.

And as the dark light
in its deep mystery tempts me
into its dim living room of trees,
lit centuries unaccountable
leading my thoughts back
into that house of the first man and woman,
I remember a young buck deer in Maine,
how we two froze in very close encounter
across a narrow path.
It was summer.
The questioning way he cocked his head,
I must've been the first human being
he'd ever seen. "Who *are* you?"
Enormous, his eyes,
their brown lights startled. It is his house now
until each second saturday in November*.

Beside the road now
where I hesitate before the open door,
bloody ribcage segments
rise as if magnified to whale
in three white arcs
like some wrecked ship
held together with blunt-end crossbars;

a macabre sky-eating sculpture.
The hide, with taupe hair,
Skillfully stripped off in one whole piece,
is draped over the remains
like a thrown-off blanket,
As if the poor beast's soul
had just got out of bed
to start its journey.

He was almost horse-high,
the buck in Maine, and his face
in its warm red squirrel red
raised in tone to red sand,
and the moistened surface
of his black nose unscarred,
held innocence immense.
A thousand miles of safe zone
could not have encompassed it.
It made us equals in surprise.
It made a fellowship of two
joined in wonder.
It seemed to take me back
into my own.
But I was long grown.
All I had was hope.
And here, now,
I still won't enter my ancient home.
I hoped so hard for the buck to live
another summer, and another,
against the vicious odds.
Call me a hypocritical fool.
Now on this gravel road

that leads so gently either way
to modern dwelling, the corner store,
I envision his bright coat
turned tawny with the season,
a color suggestive of the wisdom
he might have gained
that cannot long save him,
and I hope for him.
Not just for his kind
but for him, that individual,
in whom I saw a younger brother.
He should've had a name
for he was the poem, not the science;
whom I met face to face.

June 25, 2013 (original version Nov. 22, 2011)

Maine's rifle season dates are not Vermont's, I'm sure. I wanted the factual impact, so I gave Vermont's, these being the only dates I know. J.S.

IDENTICAL COIFFURES

The tour bus hurtled through South America at such a clip, you'd think its objective was Antarctica instead. The old madwomen who filled it had all had their hair frizzled and frazzled at some salon. Perhaps the man of each one's dreams was awaiting them in a marble pool in Patagonia. But the amazing thing was, each one had a parakeet building a nest: shaping, re-shaping their perms. The birds had flown into the bus from the rainforest in one big flock, had followed their leader through the door.

The women were in high spirits. They cackled and gobbled, some more hennish, some more turkish (meaning "like a turkey"), sometimes singly, other times in small groups, and occasionally a contagion of laughter would spread to both front and rear. These times, when up in the lower Andes, the bus itself might join in the frolic and lilt around the curves, its sides swelled pregnantly, its bussy soul lifted and guided by Pedro, the chortling driver's, brown hands.

Perhaps you would already like to know where I am going with this. Nowhere, and neither are they. I am one of these crazy ladies smiling under birds' nests. I have no idea what I'm doing on this bus. Must there be a purpose? Just call me a wordless thought, then. Call me a happiness so rootless, it has no frame of language, needs none. I'm on this bus, going everywhere and nowhere at once, for no particular reason, coiffed lovingly by a blue and green parakeet. Do you prefer analysis? Alright, then: it's the birds. They have brought the continent into the bus, whirr of feather and incessant chatter, so that all gawking ceased. With South America in the bus, there was no more need for a tour, but nobody seemed to think of that, and the big wheels kept spinning. Everyone loved the motion, and they loved the sense of no ending. That's what made this better than a ferris wheel ride. That and the avian hairdressers—of course—the main attraction.

Oh, yes, it was that bird work. In fact, it was that dirty word, unmentionable, but I will: conformity. We went rollicking all together. The parakeets' nests made all the women look alike. I was happy because I looked, at last, like everyone else. At least, I thought I did. If, in fact, my nest was not quite up to snuff; if, in reality, there was only so much a bird could do with it, I no longer minded. Eggs were laid and my nest held. Enough for me. I never noticed that the bird who chose me had flown around collecting pretzels to use in my limp hair's nest as props.

May 2013

LITTLE GRASS GHOST

The woodchuck sat up
much as we do,
on her haunches, two legs
on the ground, bent forelegs
commas in air, holding back
her body's escape run.
In the meadow's new green
that half-hid her brownness,
she scouted in place for danger,
a fat mouthful of last year's grass
headed for a nursery nest.
It sprayed yellow left and right
so that she appeared to be
not quite herself, but more
like a tussock in a marsh.
I knew that if the trapper
I hired to kill her succeeds
I will remember her thus
with all my childhood love
for a storybook animal's charm
updated to include
the shocking adult present
that never quiets, nor resolves
      its contradictions.
I'd love her still,
little grass ghost,
while harvesting my broccoli.

May 14, 2013

"MONTANA"

You said you never knew your mother.
I saw her only once or twice,
in the kitchen of your vast Victorian house
on the Academy grounds. You wanted
to introduce us, and she did say something,
but I only remember her back, quickly turned.

When your life at home became impossible,
your father drunk and vicious,
seeing his secretary,
and you came to live with Mother and me
for half the school year,
you never knew about the day
she came over to tell my mother
she just wanted to see the house,
see where you were living now,
see that you would be all right.

While you acted out at school,
setting off wind-up teeth on your desk
when the teacher bored you,
grabbing a broom to waltz with
in the girls' locker room;
being funny, getting suspended,
making straight A's without study…
one day a psychotic letter came,
addressed not in my mother's name
but to a Mrs. Peacock. It was from
an asylum in Vermont, and it spoke
of upside down green boats' houses.

It came not long past the sanity
of her visit to assure herself
of your welfare. I think the boats' houses
never turned right side up again.

Not a natural beauty, though finely boned,
you made alterations and became a bunny
in the Playboy Club. Then, aging some,
a vocal advocate for older bunnies' rights.

You even made it into Paris Match!
That club was your safe haven.
Lost investments, perhaps some dealings
with the Mafia, a trip to Kuwait
you kept a mystery, some assignment
you phoned me from in fear.
You had a baby girl to support.
Prostitution, taking on the weirdos
you wouldn't have to have sex with.

Then, always independent,
having raised yourself,
a boarder and walker of dogs
whom you leashed to furniture legs
in your small apartment in New York.
Made quite a party New Year's Eves!

Oh, the things that made us friends
that might not have
had they been otherwise:
other friends we might have had
rather than each other, if they

had only chosen us. But who else
would've begun our World Book fights,
you shouting the virtues of Montana,
I Wyoming, because you envied me
going to the Tetons for the summer,
while you stayed home? Who think up
the temporary theft of a rowboat
on Eagle Lake, that we attempted
to paddle with brooms? How else
would I have fallen from a racehorse
who burst into an unstoppable gallop
at that invisible starting gate?

My ears caked to the cochlea
with race track dirt, we gobbled
"Awful Awfuls" at the Friendly's.
You turned everything to drama,
and comedy you did best.

Near your death, your daughter said
you lost your mind, disintegrated
not only from the cancer, but I think
from the long and terrible struggle it was
to try to survive on the artifice
you might have lived well without.
I wouldn't want to have seen,
for anything, your ornery spirit
squelched, and yet

you'd have liked yourself
in a deeper sense, real, if only
the mother who came to our door
could have gone to yours.

July 9, 2013

NICE CANE

1.

How very quietly
a little, round, white life raft
on my tongue can hush
the joints of fingers, hip and knee
of their shrill complaints, and my sense
of the membrane's fragility,
        life's thread.
It's been two months of gross assault,
immune system turned against itself,
nevermore to face its foes.

I could be walking now
without my squiggle-stick
across the Hubbardton Battlefield
trying to imagine, minus success,
rows of Redcoats and Yanks
approach each other in broken ranks
across my line of sight; allowing
the field's centuries of calm
to obliterate that red riot
almost altogether,
as if there'd been no story,
or the story hadn't mattered.
Sometimes, I think, our only balm
is to hear the land itself
express itself in wordless speech,
volcano and earthquake and silence,
even if all it can tell us is ourselves

in these magnified versions
made diffuse and impersonal
in the great wash of time.

When the relief from physical pain
immediately made room today
for my daily doubts in human dealings
to start up again,
I thought of that battleground instead.

An inverted cradle now.
I willed that image. So distant…
nearly four hundred years in dandelions.
I needed to rest in those flowers.

2.

Without the Civil War, WWI, WWII,
Korea, Vietnam, Palestine & Israel,
El Salvador, Africa, Bosnia, Iran,
Iraq, Syria, Afghanistan…
      Without us,
after long patience of grass,
what new little forms might
add their shapes, lend their reasons?
But can I bear it to envision
the earth without us,
her terrible children
who fear and hate and love her so?
Yes, love, too. Look!
There's a man off-duty, fishing.
He's by himself. He hears

a thousand whispers,
many of them not ours.

Oh, the protective reflex
that shies us away so
from the seepage in
of another person's pain.
So that my aging driver
to the hospital on Friday may have
supposed I pretended,
merely chose to be helpless,
"No, no," he meant.
I won't *let* it happen to me!"

So that mangled corpses are awarded
the Bronze Star and are
so prettily be-ribboned
you'd think it's wonderful to die,
and not that loneliest of screams.

But how did I grow so smart?
Letting this prompt, careful driver
wheel me and my spiraled cane
in a chair, standard transport
while in the building, I heard,
in corridors and vast, skylit arenas,
"Nice cane!" "Nice cane!" "Nice cane!"
maybe fifteen times, to ask of me
           bravery and hope

for the better world
people try to make,
try so hard to believe in.

November 6, 2013

REUNION NEAR THE SEA

After a pleasant reunion weekend
among cousins I only met belatedly
and who seemed to me, this day,
to be all warmth and social ease,
for, indeed, there was a group heart
bound by five kids at once
on the rope swing, all
squealing their delight in the triumph,
and by the woman, over ninety,
who took her own laughing turn—
after this, for me,
a solo jaunt on the great saltwater bay,
wind and tide contending
to still me in a ginger ale light.

Then, for days back home,
my boat still rocking in the spell
of Family Reunion Day—soft inklings,
small wave-lappings, gentle proddings
in my half-conscious mind
toward happy words in new scenes
that never quite made themselves clear
so that I could remember them.

Only one image did that,
something in present time and place,
a thing I saw in the road.
As with the memories
and their would-be fresh forms,
I couldn't quite make it out

and yet my imagination
sprang on what it was, and made it so.

It was a Golden Retriever
lying in wait
beside a being in a body bag:
an ugly, heavy, black vinyl case
shaped by cording, like a garment bag
with a darker purpose. I'd wanted
to pick up the first sack
of sweet sodas and All-Love
I had put my cousins in
and take it home securely tied
to loose upon my days.

The faithful dog was waiting
for the child I'd been to waken.
As child? As elder? As what?
But the small form within that second bag
        was dead!
Yet that patient, golden head
wouldn't even lift to hear my question.

August 15, 2013

SOMEONE'S GRAM

I.

When Jill's grandmother moved her atticful
into the back yard,
it wasn't so much the broken chairs,
the hat holder like a shoe form upended,
nor even the old victrola, its propensity
to start up at midnight
and put the turntable into a spin,
with no human hand anywhere near
that bothered her so.
No, it was the infuriating way
the silver flatware pieces
in their velvet-lined wooden compartments
had begun to raise high-pitched voices
to cocktail party crescendoes
until it was like screaming
every afternoon from about four.

The narrow brook out back
talked even faster.
It seemed to challenge the members
of the party in the attic
into speech too watery and rushed
to be at all intelligible
to its gape-mouthed recipients.
"Oh!" and "Oh!" and "Oh!" they feigned,
as goldfish swam into the O's
after vacating their martinis
the way salmon leap dams.

("Olive?" asked the man tending bar.
"No, goldfish," replied the woman with
lavender hair.) Yet what Gram heard
kept turning with the turntable
into collisions of tin on tin
until her ears protested so,
she cried out in pain.

Perhaps her aged nerves
had been too frazzled over years
for her to be able to discern
anything like music
in the conversational crashes
of the tarnished silverware.
Knives, forks, spoons, corn grabbers
all sang her family history
as if it were an endless dental appointment
without novocaine. It hadn't really been
that bad. Not...*that* bad.

No! She couldn't bear it anymore.
One fine summer day, the silence
she once had relished in moments captured
from the midst of stressed, peopled days
suddenly broke up attic
into the daily four o'clock sibilance
increasing in slow degrees to cacophony
that clattered step by step
down steep rear stairs to her very feet.
Now she resolved it. Took those steps upward,
finding strength she'd thought long lost,
opened the attic window

that overlooked her deep back yard
picked up a mahogany rocking chair
whose stuffed seat housed mice,
and worked it through the opening,
and let it fall. Seven airborne mice
also found landings. Then other things,
eight hours of them, for she tired.
By midnight, there was a structure
in the yard, made of tipped chairs
roofed in tossed blankets, chimneyed
by a discard pressure cooker. Within a month,
a family of raccoons, had moved in,
as it was convenient to the garbage pails.

But then, one day, the old woman
went away, and the coons left, too.
Forsaken by her madness
by her very own hands,
deserted by her own invention
to be left in the house really alone,
she lost her mind entirely. She entered
the barren land of Catatonia,
around which an Iron Curtain fell.
There had had to be something concrete
that she could see, hear, touch—
no matter how scary, how hurtful.
Now there was nothing.
"Oh, poor soul!" wept Jill,
from far away at college;
the only one of her descendents
who had understood and loved her.
Once or twice their eyes had met

in seconds worth of true rapport.
Now she could reach her no more.

II.

Looking back,
I want to say the neighbors saw true
who said they'd watch her, dressed in green,
leave and go in her hobbit-high house
of fallen chairs, years from its dark night
or origin. I want to say Jill
had a dream that her gram, though eccentric,
clothed as she always was to blend
with the color of the yard,
returned one day to consciousness,
and that the dream came true.
Only this time,
thanks perhaps to a gentle rain
that fell in whispers as she slept,
she came to know things as they really are,
which let their beauties manifest.

December 28, 2012
& January 2, 2013

WALKING THE LAKE

I walk and walk through water.
If only
stars would fall in and swim like fish
around me;
I'd like the company. But fireflies ornament
imaginary hedges
that border each long shore. They are
the only lights
in this darkness that forgives my sins
of omission and commission
like a mother's or a father's
arms.
My feet spring me from snails like
pool balls.
My head must look bodiless floating
forward
like a breeze-driven beach ball.
I am as unattached as my head
looks
to all except these arms. At last
the causeway
and then I enter pathless forest where
the evergreens
have passed beyond their blackness to
not there.
No more fireflies! My toes become antennae
fat censors
through this night I'd always thought
I would not be able to navigate
but I am

and now I've left the forest for
the road
back to where I started from
where
a pale ghost bird lifts its wings to the
new day
and sails toward me, skimming the
brown duff
of pines. When a child I dreamt
that I
could fly, but when a bit older I was
more unsure
whether or not I had really left
the ground.
Now this bird seems to me an
apparition
its milky tone so blurred into the
dim dawn …
and instead of bothering about attaining
height
I wonder only that it took so long to know
not only
that I've always walked this blind
and managed
even when I thought I'd fallen, but that
I always will
and anything at all I might still
achieve
will come of it; out of this very dark
my light.
A robin on his highwire sang
the child

A here and now so total, so pure
sunrise alone
was in it. Miraculous! The sadness is
for such Eden
I must go not forward, but back
always back; back
to my birth in the robin's song.

Begun Jan 8, 2008
Rewrite & completion (maybe)

April 3, 2013

WHO IS THE CHILD

After a summer of not seeing you,
'chuck of many tunnels,
it is a birth to spot you again
moving from lungwort to grass.

It is a moment whose path
into my garden's destruction
is too overgrown
to believe in right away.

And for those pathless few seconds
you are as all births are:
a small, blessed miracle of lush fur
silvered across its depths.

I would take you to bed and hold you
against every horror, every plague
of hunger, yours or mine.
Who is the child?

I would protect you as if
your innocence were my aspiration;
as if I could impose my human values
to make brute nature comprehensible;

as if by traveling backwards in time
through countless early struggles
I, too, could arrive
at the unmanicured step.
I would protect you

as if innocence like yours
were mine to covet, to make
as much my own as blood on earth.

September 26, 2013

X-RAY RE-VISITED OR, ONE HEN'S DILEMMA

How little time
the Company allows for Beauty!
If poetry is only recreation
on a three-minute lake,
won't I hang up
all my eggs' membranes
on the clothes reel—
grayish, hen-sized, obscene—
and thinly enclosing little voids?

If I consider refusal
to play my part in the Company's plan
and lose thereby all connection
to my fellows in their goodness
and meanness, won't I hang up
all my eggs' membranes
void of content, just the same?
Isn't poetry
mere recreation when I *don't*
file papers for the CEO?

Oh, the hell with this. How's that
ten-minute potato in the microwave
doing, anyway?
Maybe I'll watch my eggs
turn androgynous from indecision,
become an old man's testicles—

those purple plums. Anything but have to choose. Because there is no choice, is there?

June 9, 2013

SING TO ME: A POEM OF REGRET

Who and what are you
who suck on a cloth of celery juice
      all spring
    and await fruition
of the song that gave you your lullaby,
the lullaby that gave me my song?

Are you myself?
and is it that first morning's refrain
      colored palest green
    like a forethought of living
that flowed in with the sunshine
through the slats of your crib
and on into the very cribcage
    of your little body,
and let you rest in dreams thereafter?

Oh, first the life!
The dream shall follow.

Who and what are you
that you did not take hold
    until now?
Now, in my dying time,
dropping bad apples in thuds
    upon my nerves, at last
I start to sing your song.

November 17, 2013

DESTINATION: BIRDS

Walking with you,
I don't know until we arrive,
I a little too breathless to go on,
that our objective is birds.
But here we are, eyes glued
to this spared gobbler's
ladies'-fan-not-yet,
scalloped rich umber and snow,
a crescent spread in lordship
over his adopted Muscovy ducks.

Another walk, another year
into beeches with your mother,
she saw the bark as elephant skin
and that, a perfect comparison,
brought far so near.

Now as I leave you to drive home
another outing comes to mind,
another walk. I'm not thinking
how this, too, will end at birds.
But so it does. Through the woods,
backwaters of the Ottauquechee
seen through trees, iron color
glimmering in late November light
like allure of a lost birthplace,
I come to the Raptor Center's enclosures,
bald eagles first, then the goldens.
Destination Birds, twice in a day.
I wonder, crippled creatures,

what you dream. Is it constant,
wild as you are in your cages?

Last is the snowy owl,
raised by people,
who peers at me as if this stranger
were the closest thing
to anything that she can really know,
her surrogate parents no less foreign,
her true bonds far more truly lost
than my own. What told me this?
It was the way she looked at me,
trying hard to identify, trying
with the thrust of her thick neck
and the yellow pierce of moonboat
eyes that bore so steadily
in her childishly round face
to get through to the mother *bird*.
Too many long wanders I have known
landmarks missing
and never found the poem.

Twice in one day
I've had to stop short of the river—
the Bellamy, the Ottauquechee …
only to come to understand,
my cousins, that I,
internally injured now
yet still wild in my cage,
can happen upon elephants!
Rooted, even captive
I can go anywhere.

I can find the poem.
It's an old, perhaps only human truth,
this seeing all from where one stands.
It's stale bread, a bloom of mold.
But it has become, for me
a sudden blue hydrangea.

Dec. 3, 2013

CPSIA information can be obtained
at www.ICGtesting.com
Printed in the USA
FSHW010217290721

9 781949 066708